A VINE OF VERSES

AVIKA AGARWAL

Made with ♥ on the Notion Press Platform
www.notionpress.com

‘This book is dedicated to my mom and dad, who have always support me’

Contents

Contents

Foreword

Avika Agarwal is a 12-year-old, budding author. She wrote her first book when she was 10 years old and has written many books ever since. From her books, we can see her creative and ingenious imagination and her skillfulness in poetry. Having traveled to many places such as The United States Of America and Canada, she can relate to the ambience of the places and has expressed her poetic skills, especially in this book. Unlike her other books, this book is a string of poems written by her over a period of time. She has used all types of poetry genres from which we can again see her visionary and wild imagination.

Preface

This book includes a number of poems written by the author and poet, Avika. She has included poems of different genres and categories to make sure the poems are relatable and entertaining. For easier finds, she has also separated the collections into specific categories and we hope that you enjoy reading it!

Acknowledgements

For this book, the biggest credit goes to my parents. This is because they were the ones who gave me this idea to publish a book with all my poems and they supported me and always encouraged me to write poems. The second one to thank is my sister who first introduced the concept of writing books and poems to me and it is only because of her that I was able to publish my books. Also, I'd like to thank my uncle who read all of my books and also told me ways in which I could improve my writing skills. And a big thank you to my teachers who also helped throughout the journey!

Prologue

It was a normal night in Murder Town
I was walking down the street
I walked right past the people who were
Trying to find me
I walked in the rest a room with my bloody hands
And in the mirror saw something that, I should never have
In the big brown coat that was soaked in red
He looked like he came back from the dead
With a furious look, he said
Something that made my heart race fast
In a second, my whole life had flashed
In front of me, something crashed
And there was blood on the ground
Not even a single sound...
(Continued in the book)

Poems On Festivals

1. The Deadly Night, Halloween!

October has come
Time to have fun
Dress up like monsters
Or with black fur
Halloween has come
All work is done
Paint your faces
Win comps and races
The day of the dead
It has been said
My favorite month
Not a garbage dump
Leaves Orange and red
Getting back the dead
Just enlighten your soul to the fullest
This is not a test
Don't become a bratty pest
Come to the Halloween Fest
Enlighten your soul to the fullest
Life isn't a test
Scary faces all around
Enchanting the whole town

Carving out the eyes
Is a great delight
Orange pumpkins, in fields tangled
Stems out up and jangled
Lighting up the face
After the carving race

2. The Ambience Of Thanksgiving

I am sitting outside
Sniffing the hot apple pie
Too cold to move my feet
Am only warm underneath

Aunt completed baking the hot turkey
Only the foggy steam, I had seen
I had now walked, shivering, inside
My cold gloves, now I could find

I could see the table, completed filled
With dishes, drinks, and a turkey, killed
Sweet Apple Cider, and cold winter wine
Cranberry Jam, the aroma is divine

I sat down, with a fork and spoon
Closing my eyes, sniffing the room
Cutting the turkey, a small chunk
Ate a small piece, uncle already drunk!

3. Holly Jolly Christmas Spirit!

Wish you a merry merry merry merry merry merry Christmas!
Gingerbread people are just so so delicious
Lights, shimmer, and stars are everywhere
Gift packing is opened with care
Carollers singing at my door door door
Confetti is on the bare floor floor floor
Stockings filled with precious gifts
From house to house, Santa shifts
A Christmas star at the top of the tree
Hoping for a better year for me
A half-eaten cookie on my fireplace
All the gifts wrapped with a neat lace
Footprints formed in the snow
Gifts kept, tree below
Stocking with our names on it
Me wondering why it isn't a mit
Christmas is the most wonderful time of the year
Cherish it and with your family come near

4. Happy Republic Day

Happy Republic Day, Happy Republic Day, our constitution was written
today
Dr. Bhim Rao Ambedkar helped in writing it
The British no longer rule since our people stood amidst
Mahatma Gandhi helped in making our country free
He helped us non-stop, like deep roots of a tree
Jawahar Lal Nehru also helped in making India free
He too, stood straight and helped us maintain peace
Bhagat Singh meant the same, but did it the other way
He fought with the British, and shined like a star in the middle of the
day
We are now celebrating this Republic Day
Since our constitution was written today

5. Night Time Breeze

At Night-Time
The cool and windy breeze
Runs through the town
Makes a wide and happy smile
Out of a frown
Trees swing, left to right
Breezy air running through our sleeves
Stars twinkle, a big might
Only signs of enjoyment, no grief
Short midnight strolls
In the middle of nowhere
Our curiosity does roar
About petty things we care
Looking at the constellations
In the baby blue sky
Connections between
Me and might
Then finally, get tucked into bed
Pull the blankets up to your head
Mum reads a nighttime story
And before I know it, I start snoring

6. The Month Of May

It is a brand new day
In the month, May
Sitting on the grassy hills
Mossy grass, hills are filled
The gleaming sun
Too hot just run
There is a ray of hope
You shouldn't look dope
The brand new day
It's a new start 'hey
The brand new day
A new bright ray
The brand new day
Isn't it, say?
Just live your life to the fullest
Don't live it like it's a test
Don't be a big pest
Just try to do your best
Just live your life to the fullest
The summer hills are blooming fine
Look at the sun, at its beautiful shine
The appealing flowers bloomed so soon
They look attractive like the moon
Such beauty is the best

Don't give it a rest
Have a big fest
Don't be a bad pest
Such beauty is the best…
Chirping of birds
In a soothing tree
It's not winter
Or the birds would flee
The whispering of the abandoned woods
Coming from where the birds stood
The bright sun and it's rays
The ocean and its waves
Where the bird's secret lays
When there are long days
The bright sun and its rays…

7. The Month Of June

It's finally June
Flowers ready and bloomed
Sun's bright shine,
Rays look like lines
Such a pretty rose
Watered with a hose
A beautiful evening
The telephone calls ring
Take a bath at night
Burning sun at sight
Don't get in a fight
Be in the light
Make your future bright
It is so beautiful
Instead of being dull
Birds on the tree
Tweeting cheerfully
As the sun sets
A sound sleep we get
The air cooler on
Winter's are gone
It's finally June
The birds melodious tune
It's finally June

And the big bright moon
Just enjoy the vacations
It's part of imagination

8. The Month Of July

It's already July
Get ready to ply
The brown bark of the trees
Red, yellow, and orange leaves
The sunshine is
A great delight
Soar in the sky
With a beautiful sight
It looks so beautiful
It looks very bright not dull
In the month of July
Get ready to fly
It's my favorite month
Not a garbage dump
The beautiful sun
All work is done
Enjoy your vacations
Just like your imagination
You're part of the new generation
Just have determination
The fun play-station
Enjoy your vacation…
The grassy hills
Wild-dahlias, singing merrily

AVIKA AGARWAL

Looking beautiful necessarily
The cool and windy breeze
So cold that you can freeze
Summer has finally come
Let's do some math sums

Poems On Sentiments And Feelings

9. The Arrows Of Friendship

The way you go, I am right beside
No matter if, we are in a deep slide
It does not matter
We are together

I never go, behind her back
Or speak about things that lack
In my precious friend
She is the new trend
You can say, you can say, that I sound crazy
I don't care, I don't care, if you call me lazy
I am living, I am living, my own life
I can live in my own world
Like a free kite
Cause every day, your in my heart
You and I are like an archery dart
We stick together in hardest times
I miss you, day to day
Cannot wait till we meet, hey
We will stick together in the hardest times

There is a tree we can draw
Every branch is like a straw
With our names, carved on it

The pictures that I have clicked
The ones that you have filled
Are in the tree
As you can see

10. A Broken Past

You were so happy
To finally have me
And you promised that you would never leave me
But like your cruel personality
Your promises were fake
Thought we were meant to be
But that was a mistake
And I know that you used me
But for you I feel sorry
Cause you will never know how much I really loved you
Yeah
Now when I have someone new
You just can't bear it
Eat ice-cream one spoon for two
You hate that, admit it
And you just can't get over the fact
That you are now just my past
You want to split us up so bad
You are disappointed, and that's just sad

11. Peace and War

Murky darkness takes over the skies
Sounds of wails and cries
The torment of humanity is war indeed
Abhorrence and hatred is the mere seed
In spite of war, in spite of the bloodshed
In spite of a man's suffering
I pray with all my breath
A soul within me mourns
and cries for the gone
The sky is dull, drab gray along the sea
Enlightening waves with longing for peace
Unity, we have torn into threads
It's disdain we have kept in sight
The wretched actions we then dread
Facing a shallow, dreary night
Instead, if we take the other path
Without darkness epitomizing us
Our actions no longer of wrath
No longer are we in the dust

12. What Is Wisdom?

Wisdom is a tree
It opens the path to thee
The ones who throw it back
They always have to lag
The more you spread
The more you get
Without knowledge in the world
We will be like caged birds
Our teachers help us learn
For naughty children, they have to be stern
Old have more wisdom
To learn something new is very fun
All you need is self- confidence
Be patient, don't be tense
That is common sense

13. Life, A Mystery Indeed

Life, it is just a word
But when you live it, it is a whole new world
Enjoyment and full of fun
Love and care, a ton
Family and friends, make you laugh
You are the keeper, and the staff
Nothing more, or wealthy than it
It is like a gymnasium, without a pit
Never forget, what life is worth
A proud mother has given you birth

14. Gone

I didn't know that this day would ever come in my life
I thought that everything would last forever
I thought God made us all happy
But why would he steal someone from us
He has made me so lonely
Crying on the bathroom floor
Couldn't he have warned me
So, I wouldn't have adored
Him..
But now I'm broken and shattered in pieces
No one can ever fix me, or heal it
I can't get back the time that I lost
It kills me to think, he isn't anymore
All he ever wanted was to see me succeed
But shouldn't he have known that it was him that I need?
I can't even get through a sentence without
Remembering his unfulfilled dream that I doubt
That I could ever fulfill
The small smile,
The giggle, I miss it all
I can't believe that now it's all gone
I wouldn't waste a second,
If I could do it all again
And this time, more often, I'll have said

Love you

Covering up the pain
Saying the tears are drops of water
Putting foundation on the wound
that grips me over
And over again
But now I'm broken and shattered into pieces
No one can fix me, or heal it
I can't get back the time that I lost
It kills me to think, he isn't anymore
All he ever wanted was to see me succeed
But shouldn't he have known that it was him that I need?
I can't even get through a sentence without
Remembering his dream that I doubt
I could ever fulfill
Remembering him, I'd like to say
He was the best person ever, like ever ever ever
I would lose him never never never never
NEVER EVER EVER!
Like EVER!

15. Human Kindness

Wherever we go,
Whatever our way.
We have to carry kindness in our hearts
And practice it every day.

A small smile can change our course,
Or even someone else's day.
Each simple deed creates ,
A bright sunshine ray.

A gentle touch reminds us ,
That humanity still rules.
To pat a lonely animal ,
Shows that love is cool.

Being honest kind and respectful
Is a
Little hard to be
But if we know we can do it
It will be very easy

Follow your heart and soul
Because your brain is strict
Be caring and cooperative

Even though, the path is tricked

Honesty has a million obstacles ,
On any given day
But rise above hate and fear
And live life the peaceful way.

16. What Will You Do?

What will you do, when I am not at your side?

Will you look at the ocean waves, or get washed by the tides?

When I am lost, I find my way

Will you do the same?

Stepping on a horse, Falling off of it

Which we will have to tame

Together....

Forever...

We will continue life

Until we strive

Oh oh yeah

Heavy rocks are falling from the baby blue sky

Will you cover yourself or higher you will fly

When you are going downwards, will you take me too?

Or will you tell me to stay above and wait for you?

Step on those heavy rocks and crush them so they die

Work hard to step on them, do it till they cry

Together...

Forever...

We will continue life

Life

Until we strive

Yeah,

Falling off of the cliff, will you help me up?

Or will you cut off my wings, and put them in a cup?
Will you be by my side, when I am falling off?
Or will you arrive and sit by me when I'm at the top.?
Together..
Forever…
We will continue life..
Until we strive
Will you hold me back if I am reaching high?
Or will you let go and let me fly?
On a cliff, by the sea, will you push me down?
Or will you jump and catch me before I drown?

Poems On Nature

17. Bee-Utiful Bees

Have you ever seen a big bee hive?
Do you think bees need to survive?
Yes indeed, they have to
Honey comes from them too
Collecting nectar flower to flower
Yes, I am talking about the honey we devour
They sting us because we steal it from them
The bee hive is like their den
Many different types of bees
Like porter, soldier, king, and queen
The queen produces millions of bees
Bees can fly overseas
The world's crops depend on pollination
So actually, bees also protect the nation
But they are in the danger of pollution
Let's save our food without procrastination
Together, let's protect the hives
So let's become Team HoneyFi

18. Migratory Birds All Around

Migratory birds all around
Flying from town to town
Seeking shelter everywhere
Not a person who dares
Don't burn fire crackers
Thousands of birds die
We all cause pollution
This is the reason why
Birds are so beautiful
Flying from wire to wire
Seeking peace in the trees, in the flowers
There are full of attire
Hope you all understand
The importance of this
Thank you for not causing pollution
Please try to resist
If words had wings
They would seem like birds
Together they would be like
A flock of migratory birds

19. The Relaxing Rain

Splash, Splash, Splash!
The rain drips down
Holes filling up
It is like a new town

Rain drops soothing on the rooftop
Puddles forming, drop by drop
Water pouring in the dried plants
Straight at first, then the rain slants

The relaxing sound of rain that drips
Like whipping cream, which is getting whipped
Leaves forming a little dew
Goes on like patterns of sew

I hear that leaves are drinking rain
The richer leaves are on top
Giving the poor leaves beneath
Rain, drop by drop

All night, sounds, loud and clear
Sometimes less sometimes more
Animals are hiding in fear
Catching raindrops, 3 to 4

Poems On Grandparents

20. Grandma, I Love You!

There isn't a grandma sweeter
Then just a grandma like you
You have taught me how to laugh
And find truth in everything you do
My mommy is an honest woman
Just because of you
You have given her such traits
To be responsible and love you
I hope that I can say 'Happy Grandparents Day'
Thank you for your hospitality
All along the way
You have treated me with love and care
That I can never repay

21. Our Grandparents

Grandparents are special people
With wisdom and pride
They offer a lot of love
And are always there to guide
My dad is an honest man
Just because of you
You have given him nice traits
Like to tell the truth and love you
Thank you for being side by side
In my ups and downs
For letting me get adapted
And to let me get accepted
It is because of you, that I am me today
So, why should I dedicate you, only this day
I hope that I can say 'Happy Grandparents Day'

22. A Poem On My Late Grandfather

He always held my hand, before I fell down
Always, made me happy
When I had a frown

A monkey over me, when I was in my crib
He took the paper with a pencil
And hit it with a nib

He fulfilled his duty
As a teacher, grandfather, principal, husband, and dad
Also, he never let me be sad

A loving, caring, and witty man
I think about him when I stand
Every second without him, is like being caged in a dome
It's like, a no land home

I miss him a lot
But what could I have done
When god calls someone
They just have to run

Poems On School Life

23. Nothing Better Than Books

Books are gifts
Opened many times
God's blessings and wish
Yours and mine
Read a new book,
Of any kind
Many new words
You can find
Be anywhere you want to be
Be anyone in your fantasy
Many genres- fiction and mystery
You can be a version of 'better me'
Books are our friends
And they never leave our side
Summer evening, Winter Dawn
With us, they abide
They tell us about this world
Old things and new
From modern buildings
To yarns which they sew
So keep books close to you
They help us see things from a different point of view

24. No! Exams!

My exams were really hard
Like a knife fighting a sword
I failed and got bad marks
But I will try again from the start
I thought I had disappointed mom and dad
I cried out my stomach and was super sad
But then mom said she didn't expect anything from me
She said that it was their fault, dad's and she
They are building a new house and couldn't help me study
That is why I feel better and now am happy
This has got me motivated
No one can stop me
From studying hard and opening that gate
I am also trying to lessen my screen time
For that will help me
And am trying to study
Every chapter more thoroughly
Since I want to pass my next term's exams
Wish me good luck and help me pass this program

25. School Life, A Lush

Yeah, I know that school is gonna start
And I have to play my only part
It the last day of summer
Gonna be such a bummer
I am going to sing my heart out loud
If it's a whisper or a shout
Really, I don't care
If it isn't fair
It wasn't much
And I thought it was a rush
I don't know why
But I gave up
It was a gush
All I said that was 'shush'
I don't know why
But I gave up
I know that high-school is gonna start
And I know that study is a part
Studying day and night
Gonna make my future bright
Yeah, being a freshman is my part
It's my only archery dart
To get good marks
I'll stay up till dark

Poems On The Armed Forces And

Famous Personalities

26. Salute To Captain Vikram Batra

Vikram Batra
By far the best gallantry
Who gave up his life
For this country
I want to be like him
In every possible way
His bravery, courage,
In every way, I can say
For her never wanted praise
He said it was his duty
To rescue and save
He said as a soldier
He was bound to fight
For he cared for all of our lives
Like him, I'd want to secure a child's life
Till late at night, I'd have my gun and my knife
I'd always remain loyal to orders
Spending time with the austere commander
Always lonely, it won't matter
Standing attentively at the country's border
Everyone, mostly strangers
Would be my family, in every danger

No less than my sister or brother
I would treat them like no other
Against terrorist attacks
A wall that cannot break
Whether it is cannons or bullets
I'd try my best to keep everyone safe
I do not ask for appreciation
But a thank you would make my day
I am someone's inspiration
with pride, I can say
Everyone enjoys a holiday
On Independence and Republic Day
But no one tends to remember
Because of who they are free today
So like Captain Batra
I'd go by my wits
I'd be willing to sacrifice my life
If it keeps them safe

27. The Seeds to Freedom

Let's honor our military
For the lives that are gone
For the gunshots at them
For they wake up at dawn
Let's respect them for their courage
They are ready to give up their lives
They know the dangers of going to war
Still, only some survive
Let's be like our soldiers.
We might think it's cruel
To walk in synchronization
And to follow every rule
Thank you to the soldiers,
For every drop of blood
You have been a great help
In the hardest times, you stood
If not other than our common ground to meet
Let me remember the anonymous for once at least
Beyond the patriotic floats display
On a Republic day

28. Rosa Parks, A Voice

Go to the back of the bus, Rosa Parks
Sit at the back and stay
"That is very unfair to us
And I am just too tired today"

But you will be sent to jail
For disobeying the rules
"One of us has to speak
And teach a lesson to those fools"

This is our place, go sit in the back
After all you are nothing much than a black
"I am not going to listen to you at all
Thousands of voices think the same
And this is my call"

Let us all join you Rosa Parks
You blacks don't deserve such behavior
We all will be treated equal
And will also be the savior

We are now coming to join you Rosa Parks
People, black and white did say
We are coming to change America

And bring equality today to stay

Poems On Health

29. Let's Be Fit

Do you really need that burger ?
That coke and those fries
Amidst the salt and calories
Remains a fat pack of lies

Roasted and fried in oil
Only makes you lay in bed
All the fun, that is spoilt
Makes a really dizzy head

Though eating fruits and veggies
Will make a clean you
Sitting in front of the T.V. all-day
Will bring you down, with a bad flu

So what do you think you are doing?
Why are you still here?
Go out, and be all fit
Because this is your year!!!

30. Covid-19, The Deadliest Virus

Wearing masks, using hand sanitizers
This deadly virus is a surpriser
Washing your hands all the time
People sell soaps for more than a dime
Medical bills are already high
Cures of this virus are all lies
Social distancing has kept us apart
We were better off at the start
Ayurveda recipes and modern medicines
Don't forget the doctor, working day and night like engines
Actors are heroes only in movies
We go to doctors when we are feeling woozy
Doctors are the real warriors
Between this virus and us, they are like barriers
We should try to help in any way
By not getting out, at home we stay

Poems On General Fiction And Sports

31. Welcome To Murder Town

It was a normal night in Murder Town
I was walking down the street
I walked right past the people who were
Trying to find me
I walked in the restroom with my bloody hands
And in the mirror saw something that, I should never have
In the big brown coat that was soaked in red
He looked like he came back from the dead
With a furious look, he said
Something that made my heart race fast
In a second, my whole life had flashed
In front of me, something crashed
And there was blood on the ground
Not even a single sound
There he was lying, in blood, drowned
And a drop fell on me
Slid down slowly
I look up and I see
There she was,
My partner in crime
Been friends since we were nine
While watching the stars, we saw a shine

And that is how we
GOT STUCK IN TIME!

32. Gymnastics, A Feeling

Cartwheels Cartwheels, all around
Flipping now up and down
Sprained ankle, does not matter
Leaving it is even sadder

Competition of only minutes
Practice for a whole year
No matter if it goes waste
You still tried, without any fear

Aerials, Cartwheels, and even flips
You learned them, with many slips
Even if you had a fracture
You never stopped learning to capture

Balancing on the beams
That is one lovely skill
Cheerful and full of energy
You go around like a windmill

No matter, how old you are
There is no age for it
Swirling around that bar
In a unitard, lit!

Climbing on the rope of hope
Falling down in the pit
Going up again
That is the spirit!

33. Cricket, All About Sixes!

Cricket is an overwhelming sport
That includes a ball hitting a bat
You swing your arms high and low
Some people on the bench, they sat

T20 matches are happening this week
Cricketers hitting sixes and fours
Audience from the seats they seek
People want some sixes more

When the hit gets caught
Everyone watches in suspense
When the referee declares an out
Everyone begins to get tense

Today is RCB and KKR's match
The ballers are practicing their spins
People with their TV are attached
To watch them hit with their fin

Pant, Rishab, Dhoni do their best
Catch the balls on the field
They get only an hour of rest
And wear a helmet to shield

All the teams are great
Whether they qualify or not
No matter if it is DC or RR
The teams have been bought

You can root for your own team
And I will root for mine
Want to bet on who will win?
I can put a dime

Copycats Collection

34. Copycats (Copycats 1)

I have my own identity and accomplishments
I have made a little money which I am free to spend
Be Jealous
I don't care
Copy me
I can share
Nice, in front of the teacher
Inside, you're a cheater
Yeah, yeah, yeah, yeah, a cheater
(Hum hum) Chea-ter
You don't have a face of your own
Take me down, I don't moan
Cause' I know I'm better than you
And I know that you know too
You are nothing more than copycat
Selfish cause' I am there, where you sat
Copycat
Selfish Rat
I have a magic mat
You bat!

35. A Response To Copycats (Copycats 2)

I have a real identity and accomplishments
I have made a ton of money which I am free to spend
Ask google, it knows who I am
Check YouTube, plus 20,000 fans
English Teacher, adores me
That clearly we all can see
(Mmmhmmhmmmhmm) Is that Jealousy?
(Mmmhmmh) Jealousy!
Many article in The Global TImes
So many that I can't count mine
Only two brags like thousand
You wanted praise, have you found it?
You are so intimidated
No real talent, you have to fake it
Try to act like you are doing good
But honey not a chance in your childhood
And with my talent, the war is unfair
Remember I am your worst nightmare
Cause' you are nothing more than a COPYCAT!
Jealous cause' I am there where you sat
Jealous, Selfish, Copycat
I have many friends with who I chat

But you might feel bad to hear this
But you are not on my friends list
(Mmhmmhmmhmm) Is that a tear?
(Mmhmm) Do I smell fear?
I innovate and I inspire
You are a big admirer
Try to master every move of mine
Go on, honey, I'd like to see your try
But you are nothing more than a COPYCAT
Jealous cause' I am there where you sat
Copycat, Jealous Rat
You are good,
But in the nice list the last!

About The Author

Avika Agarwal

Avika Agarwal is a budding 12-year-old author and poetess. She started writing at the age of 10 and has written many books till now. Her books are a way for her to express her creativity and imagination in different ways. Her books have always left the audience astonished about how a young girl can write such beautiful poems, songs, and mysterious books. Since she has lived in the United States Of America and Canada, she knows different lifestyles and can compose poems about her experiences. She is an enthusiastic girl who loves reading, writing, drawing, and singing. And she has combined all her hobbies, together, in this special book. For listening to her songs, you can visit her YouTube channel, The Craftivity Show, and watch the playlist, 'Songs'. Hope you loved her poems and have a sublime day!

www.ingramcontent.com/pod-product-compliance
Lightning Source LLC
Chambersburg PA
CBHW031453150726
47990CB00007B/2742